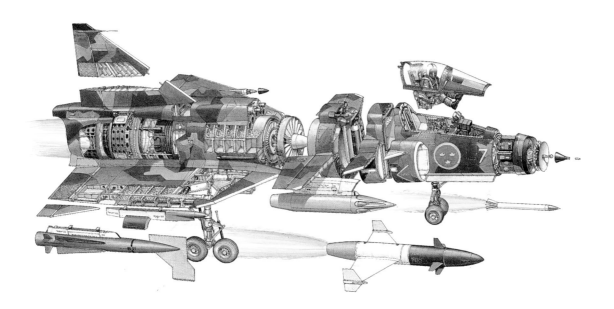

LOOK INSIDE
CROSS-SECTIONS
JETS

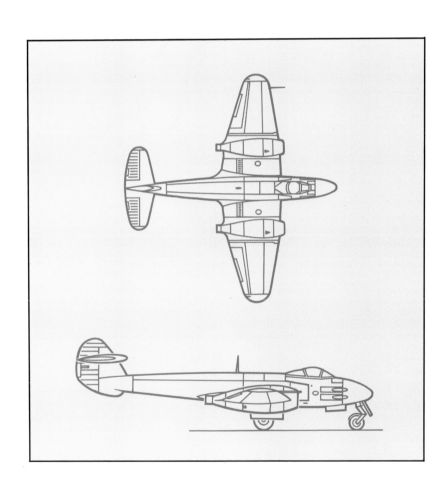

LOOK INSIDE
CROSS-SECTIONS
JETS

ILLUSTRATED BY
HANS JENSSEN
WRITTEN BY
MOIRA BUTTERFIELD

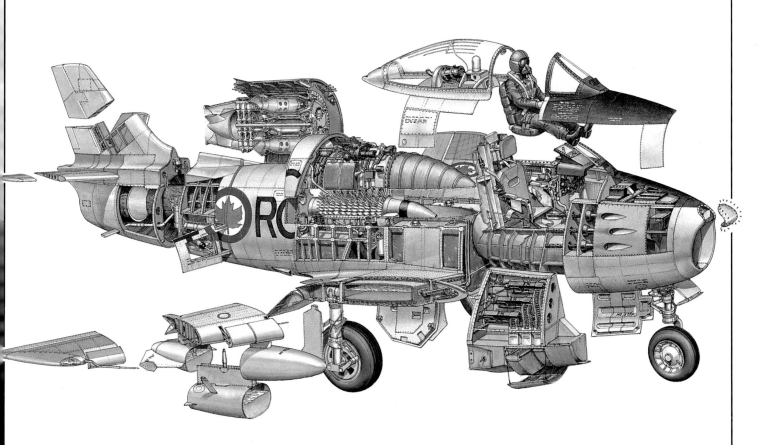

A DK PUBLISHING BOOK
www.dk.com

Senior Art Editor Dorian Spencer Davies
Designer Joanne Earl
Senior Editor John C. Miles
Editorial Assistant Nigel Ritchie
U.S. Editor Camela Decaire
Deputy Art Director Miranda Kennedy
Deputy Editorial Director Sophie Mitchell
Production Charlotte Traill
Consultant Andrew Nahum
The Science Museum, London

First American edition, 1996
4 6 8 10 9 7 5 3
Published in the United States
by DK Publishing, Inc.,
95 Madison Avenue, New York, New York 10016

**A CIP catalog record is available
from the Library of Congress**

ISBN: 0-7894-0767-1

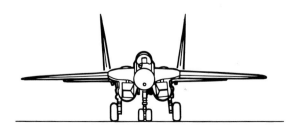

Reproduced by Dot Gradations. Essex
Printed and bound in Belgium by Proost

CONTENTS

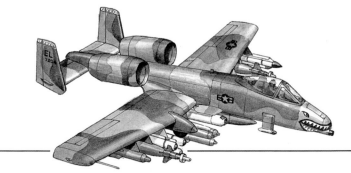

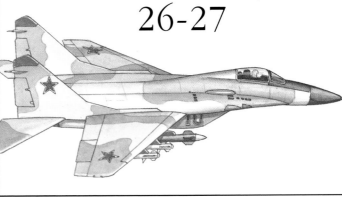
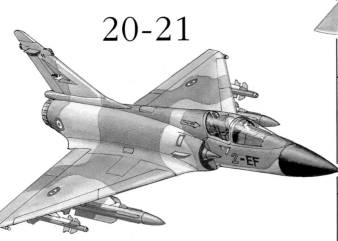

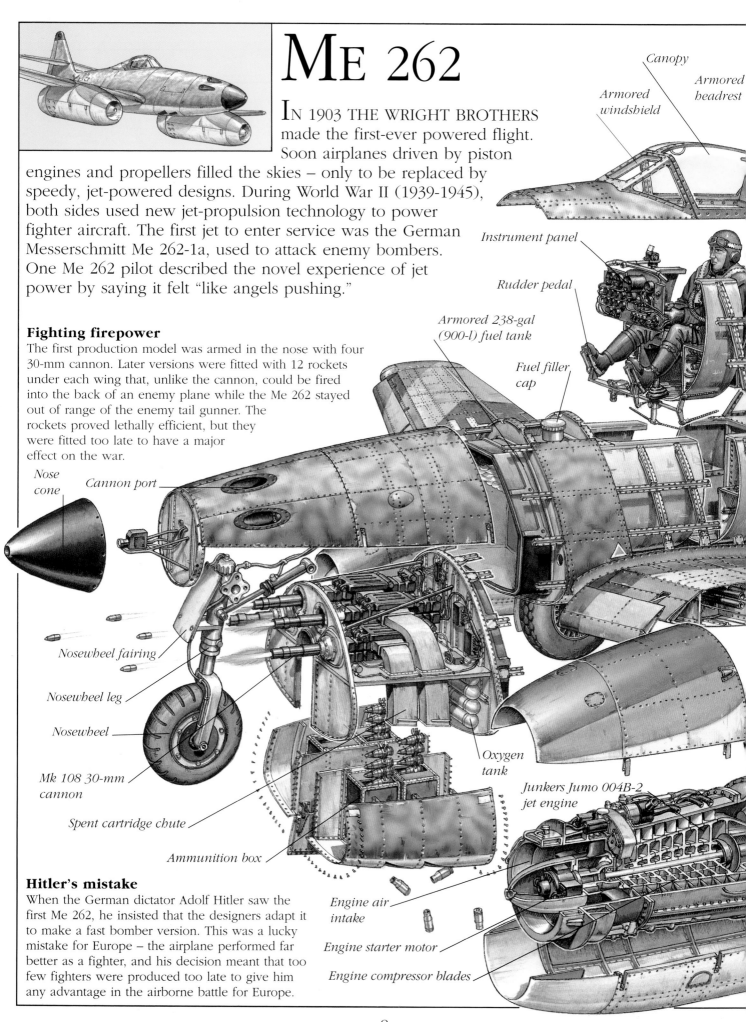

Me 262

In 1903 THE WRIGHT BROTHERS made the first-ever powered flight. Soon airplanes driven by piston engines and propellers filled the skies – only to be replaced by speedy, jet-powered designs. During World War II (1939-1945), both sides used new jet-propulsion technology to power fighter aircraft. The first jet to enter service was the German Messerschmitt Me 262-1a, used to attack enemy bombers. One Me 262 pilot described the novel experience of jet power by saying it felt "like angels pushing."

Fighting firepower

The first production model was armed in the nose with four 30-mm cannon. Later versions were fitted with 12 rockets under each wing that, unlike the cannon, could be fired into the back of an enemy plane while the Me 262 stayed out of range of the enemy tail gunner. The rockets proved lethally efficient, but they were fitted too late to have a major effect on the war.

Hitler's mistake

When the German dictator Adolf Hitler saw the first Me 262, he insisted that the designers adapt it to make a fast bomber version. This was a lucky mistake for Europe – the airplane performed far better as a fighter, and his decision meant that too few fighters were produced too late to give him any advantage in the airborne battle for Europe.

Canopy

Armored windshield

Armored headrest

Instrument panel

Rudder pedal

Armored 238-gal (900-l) fuel tank

Fuel filler cap

Nose cone

Cannon port

Nosewheel fairing

Nosewheel leg

Nosewheel

Mk 108 30-mm cannon

Spent cartridge chute

Ammunition box

Oxygen tank

Junkers Jumo 004B-2 jet engine

Engine air intake

Engine starter motor

Engine compressor blades

TECHNICAL DATA

LENGTH:
34 FT 10 IN (10.6 M)

HEIGHT:
12 FT 8 IN (3.9 M)

WINGSPAN:
41 FT (12.5 M)

MAX SPEED:
541 MPH (870 KM/H)

ARMAMENT:
4 RHEINMETALL-BORSIG
MK 108 CANNON

ENGINES:
2 JUNKERS JUMO 004B-2 TURBOJETS

Jump and hope

During the war many pilots flew the airplane without any special jet training; they had to learn how to handle the aircraft on the job. If they needed to bail out, they pulled a lever to make the canopy fly off. Then they jumped – and hoped their parachute would open!

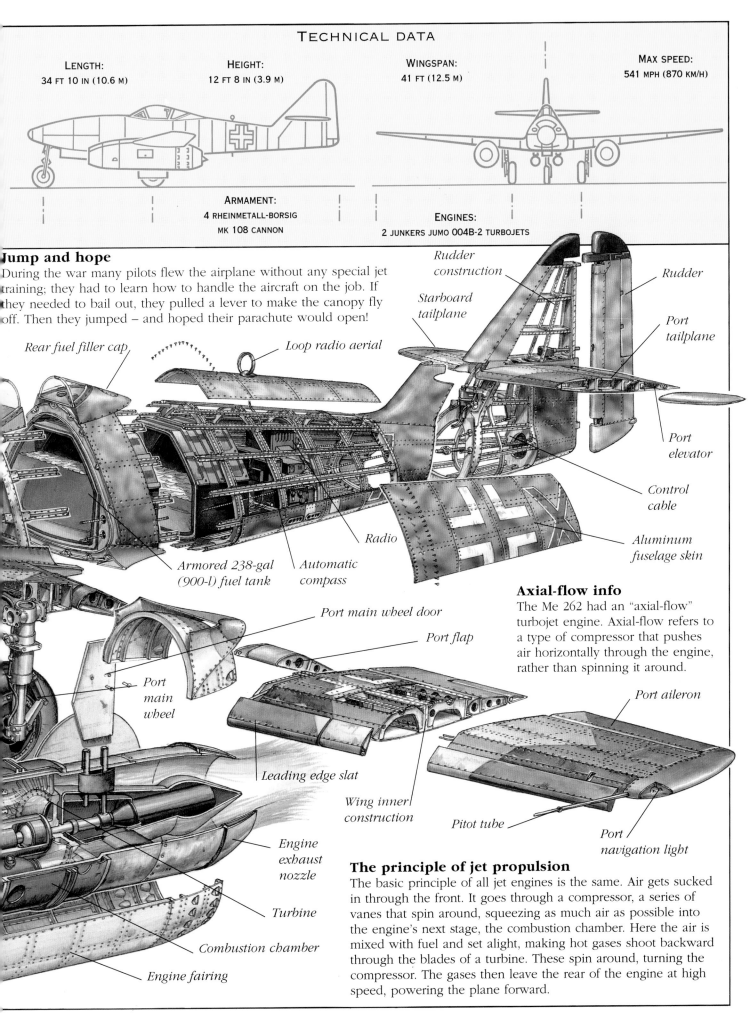

Rudder construction

Starboard tailplane

Rudder

Port tailplane

Port elevator

Control cable

Aluminum fuselage skin

Rear fuel filler cap

Loop radio aerial

Radio

Armored 238-gal (900-l) fuel tank

Automatic compass

Port main wheel door

Port flap

Port main wheel

Leading edge slat

Wing inner construction

Pitot tube

Port aileron

Port navigation light

Engine exhaust nozzle

Turbine

Combustion chamber

Engine fairing

Axial-flow info

The Me 262 had an "axial-flow" turbojet engine. Axial-flow refers to a type of compressor that pushes air horizontally through the engine, rather than spinning it around.

The principle of jet propulsion

The basic principle of all jet engines is the same. Air gets sucked in through the front. It goes through a compressor, a series of vanes that spin around, squeezing as much air as possible into the engine's next stage, the combustion chamber. Here the air is mixed with fuel and set alight, making hot gases shoot backward through the blades of a turbine. These spin around, turning the compressor. The gases then leave the rear of the engine at high speed, powering the plane forward.

9

GLOSTER METEOR

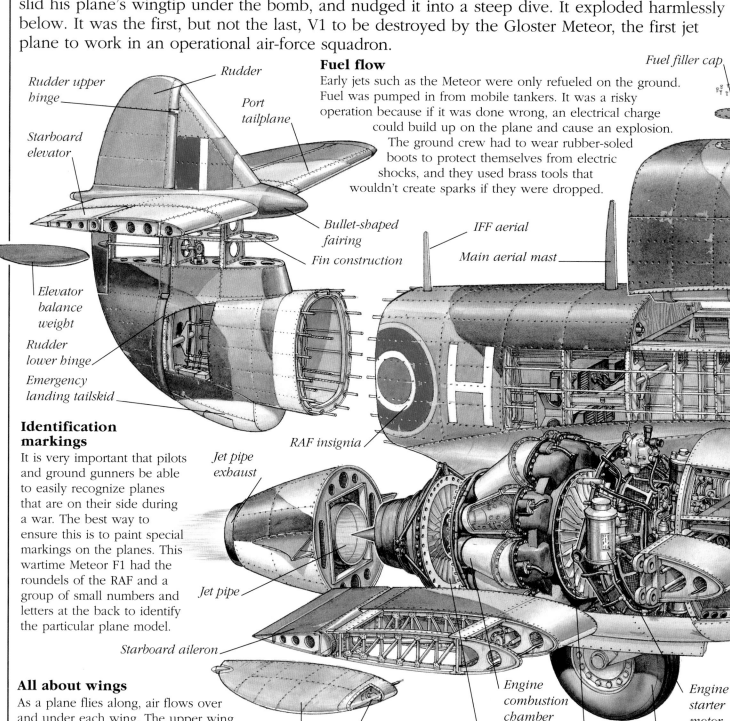

ON A SUMMER DAY IN 1944 FLIGHT OFFICER "Dixie" Dean of Britain's Royal Air Force made aviation history. In a brand-new plane developed by the pioneering design team of Frank Whittle and George Carter, Dean spotted a deadly V1 flying bomb speeding over the south coast of England toward London. He fired the plane's cannons, but they jammed. Desperate, he flew alongside, slid his plane's wingtip under the bomb, and nudged it into a steep dive. It exploded harmlessly below. It was the first, but not the last, V1 to be destroyed by the Gloster Meteor, the first jet plane to work in an operational air-force squadron.

Fuel flow

Early jets such as the Meteor were only refueled on the ground. Fuel was pumped in from mobile tankers. It was a risky operation because if it was done wrong, an electrical charge could build up on the plane and cause an explosion. The ground crew had to wear rubber-soled boots to protect themselves from electric shocks, and they used brass tools that wouldn't create sparks if they were dropped.

Identification markings

It is very important that pilots and ground gunners be able to easily recognize planes that are on their side during a war. The best way to ensure this is to paint special markings on the planes. This wartime Meteor F1 had the roundels of the RAF and a group of small numbers and letters at the back to identify the particular plane model.

All about wings

As a plane flies along, air flows over and under each wing. The upper wing surface is curved, and the air flowing over it has a lower pressure than the air traveling past the flat surface under the wing. The air beneath pushes upward with a force called "upthrust," giving the plane enough "lift" to stay airborne.

Rudder upper hinge

Rudder

Port tailplane

Starboard elevator

Bullet-shaped fairing

Fin construction

Fuel filler cap

IFF aerial

Main aerial mast

Elevator balance weight

Rudder lower hinge

Emergency landing tailskid

RAF insignia

Jet pipe exhaust

Jet pipe

Starboard aileron

Starboard navigation light

Starboard detachable wingtip

Engine combustion chamber

Engine turbine blades

Compressor blades

Engine starter motor

Starboard main wheel

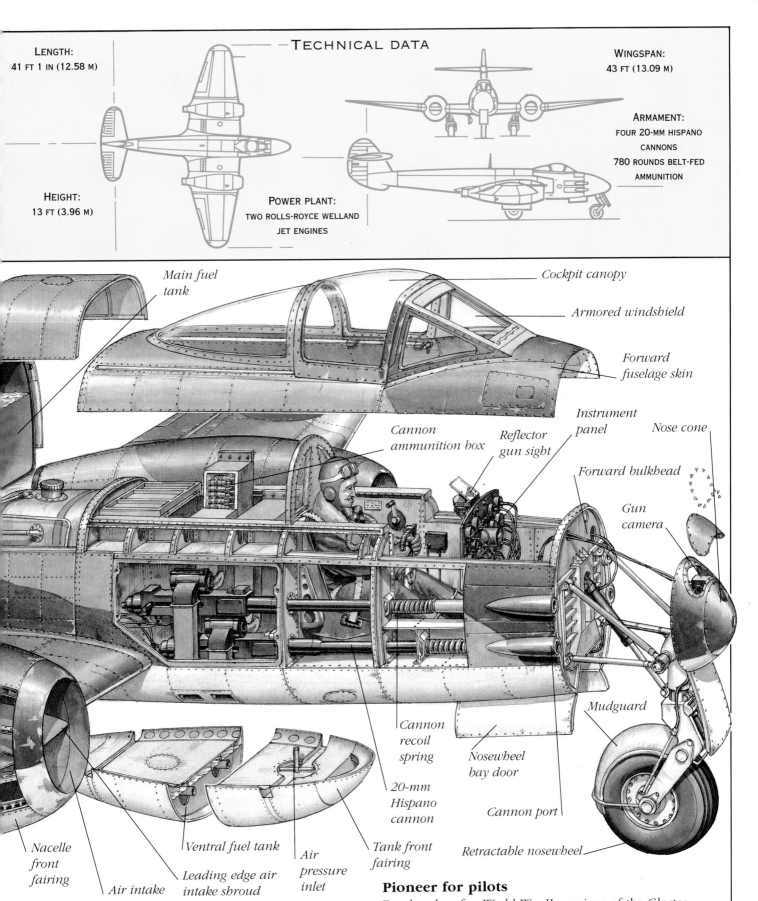

LENGTH:
41 FT 1 IN (12.58 M)

HEIGHT:
13 FT (3.96 M)

POWER PLANT:
TWO ROLLS-ROYCE WELLAND
JET ENGINES

WINGSPAN:
43 FT (13.09 M)

ARMAMENT:
FOUR 20-MM HISPANO
CANNONS
780 ROUNDS BELT-FED
AMMUNITION

Main fuel tank

Cockpit canopy

Armored windshield

Forward fuselage skin

Instrument panel

Cannon ammunition box

Reflector gun sight

Nose cone

Forward bulkhead

Gun camera

Cannon recoil spring

20-mm Hispano cannon

Nosewheel bay door

Cannon port

Mudguard

Retractable nosewheel

Tank front fairing

Nacelle front fairing

Air intake

Ventral fuel tank

Leading edge air intake shroud

Air pressure inlet

Flying features

The Meteor F1 had four cannons mounted in the front fuselage, three wheels on the "tricycle" landing gear, a tailplane set high up at the back, and two engines mounted on the wings. Each engine was fitted inside a streamlined metal casing called a nacelle.

Pioneer for pilots

For decades after World War II, versions of the Gloster Meteor were used by air forces all over the world. Many young pilots got their first jet training in a Meteor and models were often used to test out new equipment such as ejection seats. In the decade after the war, a succession of Meteors held the world airspeed record, flying at more than 600 mph (990 km/h).

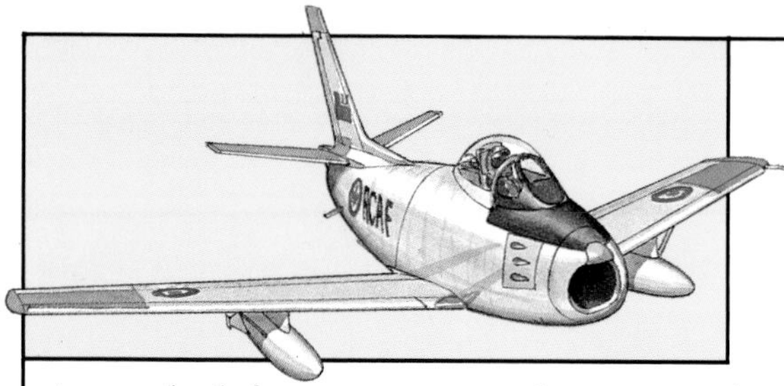

F-86 SABRE

THE DESIGN THAT BECAME THE US F-86 SABRE originated in World War II. However, this fighter was not intended for service in the war. The North American Aviation company wanted its designers to use technology gleaned from captured German aircraft. The wait paid off. The prototype (first) Sabre flew on October 1, 1947. Three years later, developed versions saw combat in the Korean War (1950-53). After the Korean War, versions of the F-86 were bought by many countries, and remained in service throughout the 1960s. The picture below shows a Canadair Sabre 6 of the Royal Canadian Air Force.

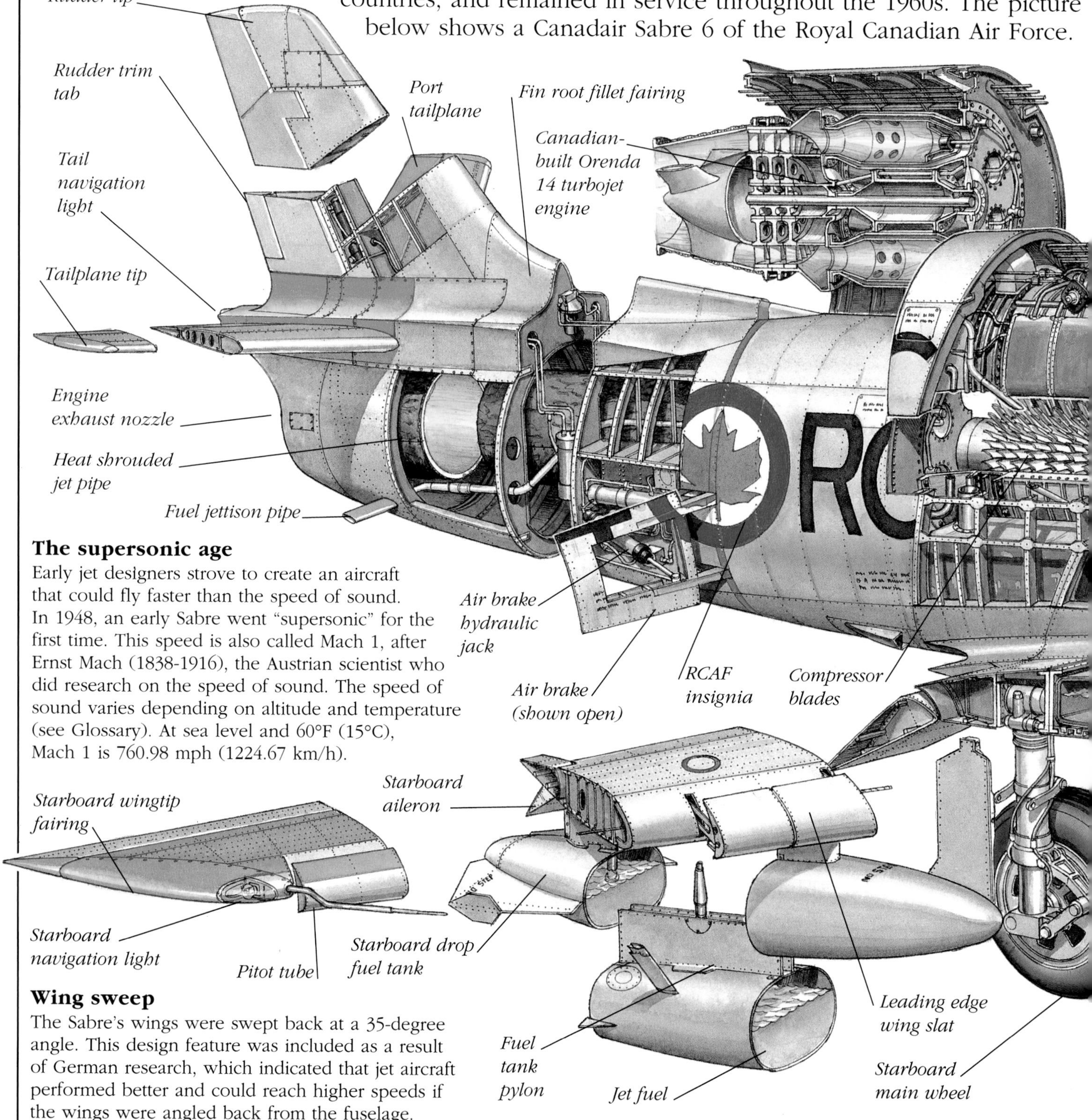

Rudder tip

Rudder trim tab

Port tailplane

Fin root fillet fairing

Canadian-built Orenda 14 turbojet engine

Tail navigation light

Tailplane tip

Engine exhaust nozzle

Heat shrouded jet pipe

Fuel jettison pipe

Air brake hydraulic jack

Air brake (shown open)

RCAF insignia

Compressor blades

The supersonic age

Early jet designers strove to create an aircraft that could fly faster than the speed of sound. In 1948, an early Sabre went "supersonic" for the first time. This speed is also called Mach 1, after Ernst Mach (1838-1916), the Austrian scientist who did research on the speed of sound. The speed of sound varies depending on altitude and temperature (see Glossary). At sea level and 60°F (15°C), Mach 1 is 760.98 mph (1224.67 km/h).

Starboard wingtip fairing

Starboard aileron

Starboard navigation light

Pitot tube

Starboard drop fuel tank

Leading edge wing slat

Starboard main wheel

Fuel tank pylon

Jet fuel

Wing sweep

The Sabre's wings were swept back at a 35-degree angle. This design feature was included as a result of German research, which indicated that jet aircraft performed better and could reach higher speeds if the wings were angled back from the fuselage.

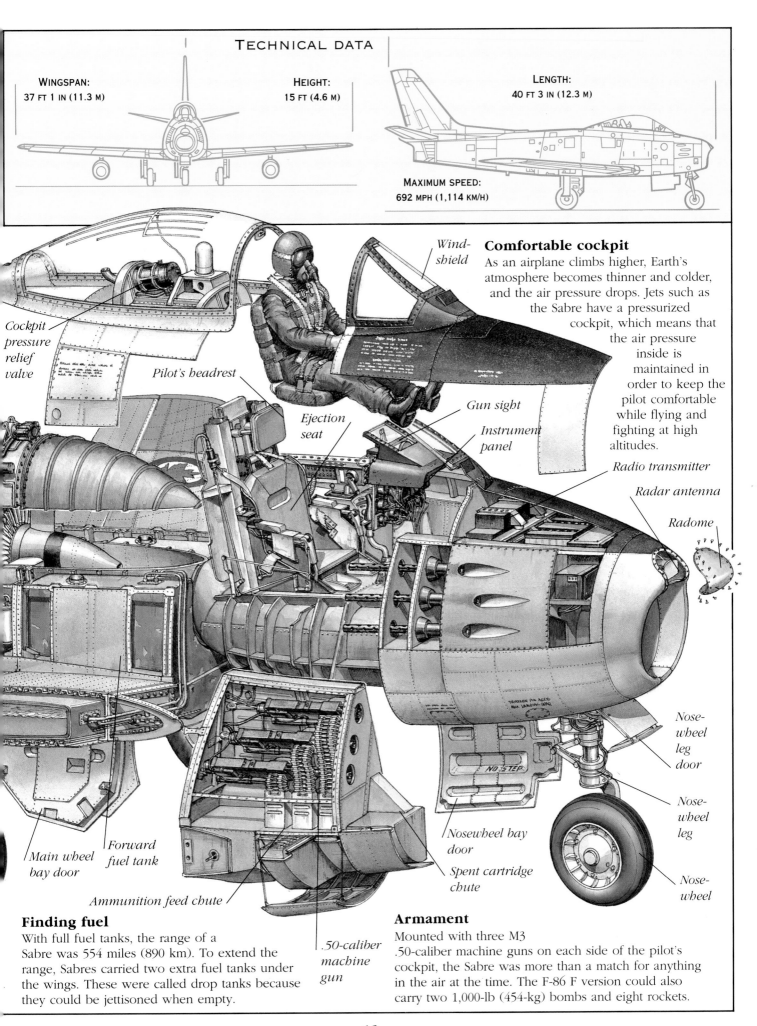

TECHNICAL DATA

WINGSPAN:
37 FT 1 IN (11.3 M)

HEIGHT:
15 FT (4.6 M)

LENGTH:
40 FT 3 IN (12.3 M)

MAXIMUM SPEED:
692 MPH (1,114 KM/H)

Cockpit pressure relief valve

Pilot's headrest

Ejection seat

Wind-shield

Gun sight

Instrument panel

Comfortable cockpit

As an airplane climbs higher, Earth's atmosphere becomes thinner and colder, and the air pressure drops. Jets such as the Sabre have a pressurized cockpit, which means that the air pressure inside is maintained in order to keep the pilot comfortable while flying and fighting at high altitudes.

Radio transmitter

Radar antenna

Radome

Nose-wheel leg door

Nose-wheel leg

Nose-wheel

Main wheel bay door

Forward fuel tank

Ammunition feed chute

.50-caliber machine gun

Nosewheel bay door

Spent cartridge chute

Finding fuel

With full fuel tanks, the range of a Sabre was 554 miles (890 km). To extend the range, Sabres carried two extra fuel tanks under the wings. These were called drop tanks because they could be jettisoned when empty.

Armament

Mounted with three M3 .50-caliber machine guns on each side of the pilot's cockpit, the Sabre was more than a match for anything in the air at the time. The F-86 F version could also carry two 1,000-lb (454-kg) bombs and eight rockets.

A-10 THUNDERBOLT

ONE OF THE MOST UNUSUAL JET AIRCRAFT EVER CREATED, the strange looks of the A-10 Thunderbolt have led to its being nicknam "Warthog," after a kind of wild pig renowned for being ugly and fierce! Developed in the 1970s, the plane is still being used by the US military. Like its animal namesake, the A-10 forages near the ground. It is equipped with a formidable array of weapons and cruises above a battlefield at low altitude, searching for enemy tanks. Once an enemy tank is located, the pilot destroys it with the plane's rapid-fire 30-mm cannon or its air-to-ground missiles

Extra armor

Inside the cockpit, the pilot is surrounded by super strong titanium-alloy armor up to 1.5 in (38 mm) thick. This protects the pilot against hits from the ground when the "Warthog" is flying in low to attack a tank.

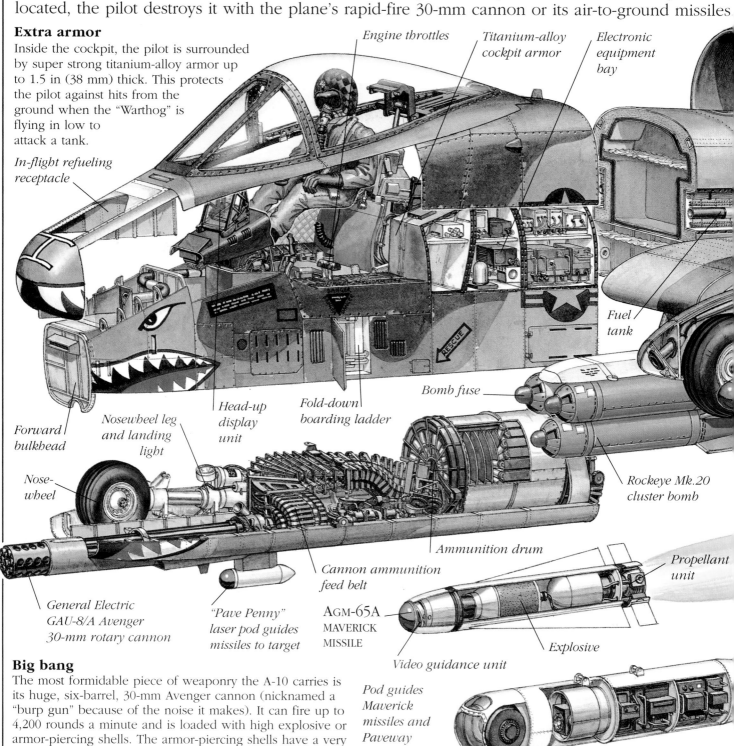

Engine throttles

Titanium-alloy cockpit armor

Electronic equipment bay

In-flight refueling receptacle

Fuel tank

Bomb fuse

Forward bulkhead

Nosewheel leg and landing light

Head-up display unit

Fold-down boarding ladder

Rockeye Mk.20 cluster bomb

Nose-wheel

General Electric GAU-8/A Avenger 30-mm rotary cannon

"Pave Penny" laser pod guides missiles to target

Cannon ammunition feed belt

Ammunition drum

Propellant unit

AGM-65A MAVERICK MISSILE

Explosive

Video guidance unit

Big bang

The most formidable piece of weaponry the A-10 carries is its huge, six-barrel, 30-mm Avenger cannon (nicknamed a "burp gun" because of the noise it makes). It can fire up to 4,200 rounds a minute and is loaded with high explosive or armor-piercing shells. The armor-piercing shells have a very dense uranium core, that enables them to blast through armor plates on enemy tanks.

Pod guides Maverick missiles and Paveway bombs to targets on ground

LANTIRN TARGETING POD

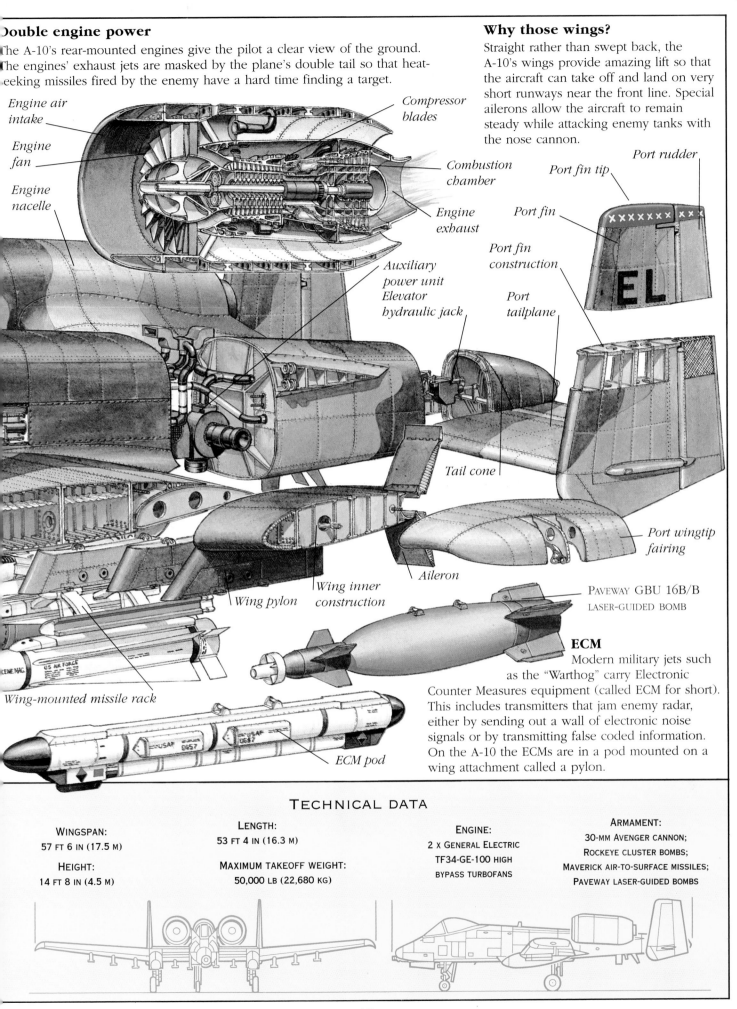

Double engine power

The A-10's rear-mounted engines give the pilot a clear view of the ground. The engines' exhaust jets are masked by the plane's double tail so that heat-seeking missiles fired by the enemy have a hard time finding a target.

Engine air intake

Engine fan

Engine nacelle

Compressor blades

Combustion chamber

Engine exhaust

Auxiliary power unit
Elevator hydraulic jack

Wing inner construction

Wing pylon

Wing-mounted missile rack

ECM pod

Why those wings?

Straight rather than swept back, the A-10's wings provide amazing lift so that the aircraft can take off and land on very short runways near the front line. Special ailerons allow the aircraft to remain steady while attacking enemy tanks with the nose cannon.

Port rudder

Port fin tip

Port fin

Port fin construction

Port tailplane

Tail cone

Port wingtip fairing

Aileron

PAVEWAY GBU 16B/B
LASER-GUIDED BOMB

ECM

Modern military jets such as the "Warthog" carry Electronic Counter Measures equipment (called ECM for short). This includes transmitters that jam enemy radar, either by sending out a wall of electronic noise signals or by transmitting false coded information. On the A-10 the ECMs are in a pod mounted on a wing attachment called a pylon.

TECHNICAL DATA

WINGSPAN: 57 FT 6 IN (17.5 M)	LENGTH: 53 FT 4 IN (16.3 M)	ENGINE: 2 X GENERAL ELECTRIC TF34-GE-100 HIGH BYPASS TURBOFANS	ARMAMENT: 30-MM AVENGER CANNON; ROCKEYE CLUSTER BOMBS; MAVERICK AIR-TO-SURFACE MISSILES; PAVEWAY LASER-GUIDED BOMBS
HEIGHT: 14 FT 8 IN (4.5 M)	MAXIMUM TAKEOFF WEIGHT: 50,000 LB (22,680 KG)		

STARFIGHTER

THE MISSILE-SHAPED LOCKHEED F-104 STARFIGHTER originated in the Korean War (1950-53). The chief designer at Lockheed, C.L. "Kelly" Johnson, talked to pilots returning from the war. He began to design a jet fighter for the US Air Force based on the pilots' thoughts. The aircraft that emerged four years later was faster than anything flown by enemy forces, with wings only 4 in (10 cm) thick to reduce drag (air resistance) at supersonic speeds. Early versions of the Starfighter were dogged by accidents and a high crash rate, but later versions were more successful and were bought by countries such as Germany, Italy, Canada, and Japan for their air forces.

HUD

Some Starfighter versions were among the first planes to be fitted with head-up display (HUD for short) in the cockpit. In a jet fighter with HUD, vital information from the control dials and displays is projected onto the windshield, so the pilot does not have to look down while flying.

Unusual ejection

The first F-104s were fitted with a downward-firing ejector seat, because the more usual upward-firing version might have hit the extra-high tailplane. If a pilot needs to eject, he must grab for a handle. In a split second the seat's gun cartridge fires to propel it out of the plane.

All about missiles

Missiles fired by aircraft fall into two categories. Jets fire air-to-air missiles at other jets to destroy them. The Starfighter carried up to four Sidewinder air-to-air missiles. These were heat-seeking: the missiles homed in on the enemy aircraft's hot exhaust jet. Aircraft also fire air-to-ground missiles. These destroy enemy targets on the ground below and are now usually directed by lasers to their target.

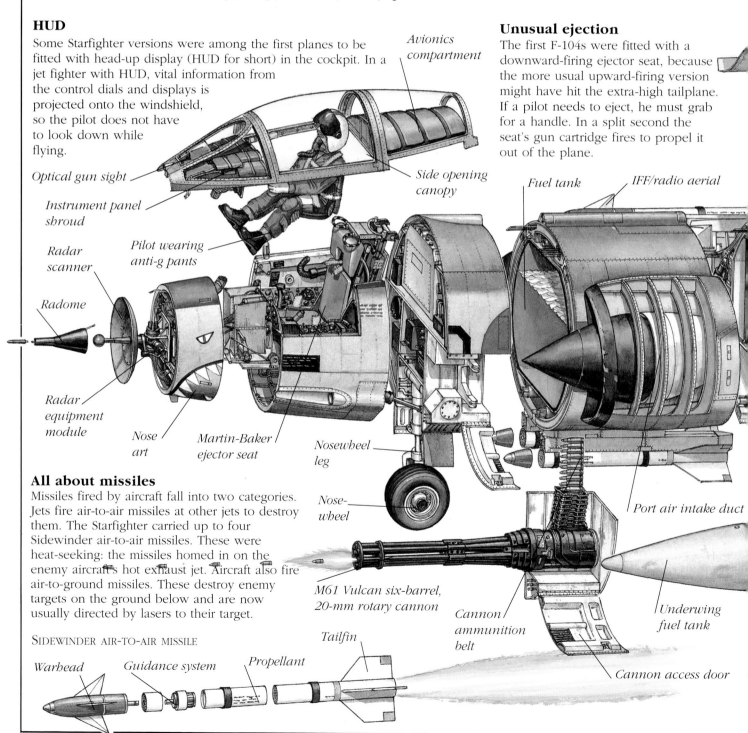

Avionics compartment

Optical gun sight

Instrument panel shroud

Radar scanner

Radome

Radar equipment module

Nose art

Martin-Baker ejector seat

Pilot wearing anti-g pants

Side opening canopy

Fuel tank

IFF/radio aerial

Nosewheel leg

Nosewheel

Port air intake duct

M61 Vulcan six-barrel, 20-mm rotary cannon

Cannon ammunition belt

Underwing fuel tank

Cannon access door

SIDEWINDER AIR-TO-AIR MISSILE

Warhead

Guidance system

Propellant

Tailfin

TECHNICAL DATA

WINGSPAN:
21 FT 11 IN (6.7 M)

HEIGHT:
13 FT 6 IN (4.2 M)

LENGTH:
54 FT 9 IN (16.7 M)

MAXIMUM SPEED:
1,300 MPH (2,092 KM/H)

ENGINE:
ONE GENERAL ELECTRIC J79-GE-19
AFTERBURNING TURBOJET

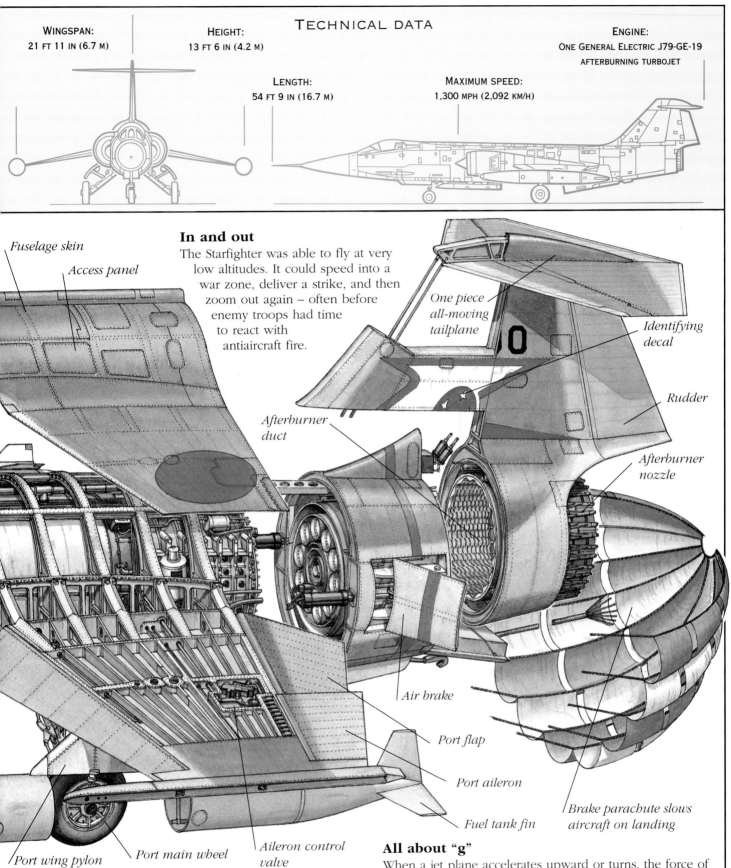

In and out

The Starfighter was able to fly at very low altitudes. It could speed into a war zone, deliver a strike, and then zoom out again – often before enemy troops had time to react with antiaircraft fire.

Fuselage skin

Access panel

One piece all-moving tailplane

Identifying decal

Rudder

Afterburner duct

Afterburner nozzle

Air brake

Port flap

Port aileron

Fuel tank fin

Brake parachute slows aircraft on landing

Port wing pylon

Port main wheel

Aileron control valve

Speedy engine

Early jet engines lacked the power to push aircraft to the speed of sound. When C.L. Johnson began to design the F-104 in the early 1950s, there was no jet engine powerful enough to reach the speeds he envisioned. Fortunately, General Electric was developing the powerful J79 turbojet at the same time, and this became the engine of the F-104.

All about "g"

When a jet plane accelerates upward or turns, the force of gravity pulls down harder on the plane and the pilot. This causes a force on the body called "g." Without the right clothing, the pilot would black out because "g" stops blood from circulating properly. To prevent this, a jet pilot wears "anti-g" pants, which contain inflatable pads. The pants are attached to an air supply and the pads inflate to force blood back up to the heart.

PHANTOM

IMAGINE BEING IN A JET PLANE ZOOMING STRAIGHT UPWARD UNTIL you are nearly in space, where there is not enough air for the plane's engines to work. Then imagine plummeting back down, powerless, waiting to restart the engines. In 1959 an early Phantom pilot did just that to break the world altitude record. The F-4 two-seater version of the Phantom (first flown in 1967) went into operation with the US Navy and Marines, and was later sold to many other countries. It was designed for air-to-air combat and ground strikes, and it relied on the most up-to-date electronics of the time.

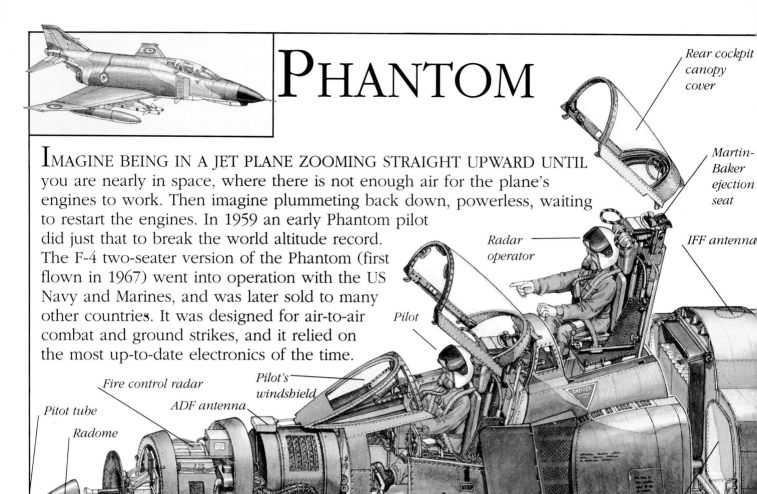

Rear cockpit canopy cover

Martin-Baker ejection seat

IFF antenna

Radar operator

Pilot

Pilot's windshield

Fire control radar

ADF antenna

Pitot tube

Radome

Gun muzzle fairing

Radar scanner

M61A-1 20-mm rotary barrel cannon

Landing and taxiing lights

Nosewheel door

Port intake duct

Sparrow missile

SIDEWINDER MISSILE

Guidance system

Nose cone

Warhead

CUTAWAY OF EXTERNAL FUEL TANK CAPACITY: 301 US GAL (1,140 L)

CUTAWAY OF SPARROW MISSILE

Stabilizer

Tailfin

Bone dome

Every jet pilot has a personally fitted helmet, nicknamed a "bone dome." The inside is comfortably padded with a communications receiver, and an outside visor slides up and down. Attached to the helmet is an oxygen mask with a built-in microphone that the pilot must wear at all times during flight. It is connected to the plane's oxygen system and to the ejector-seat emergency oxygen pack.

Top gun

The Phantom F-4 had many exciting capabilities. For instance, it could climb 49,800 ft (15,179 m) a minute and reach above Mach 2 speed at altitude. When the famous "Top Gun" American jet pilot course began, the first "Top Guns," the best young pilots in the US Navy, completed the course using Phantom F-4s.

Deadly sparrow

The AIM Sparrow air-to-air missile is a tactical radar-homing missile propelled by solid fuel. The guidance system uses infra-red sensors to locate the target's radar system.

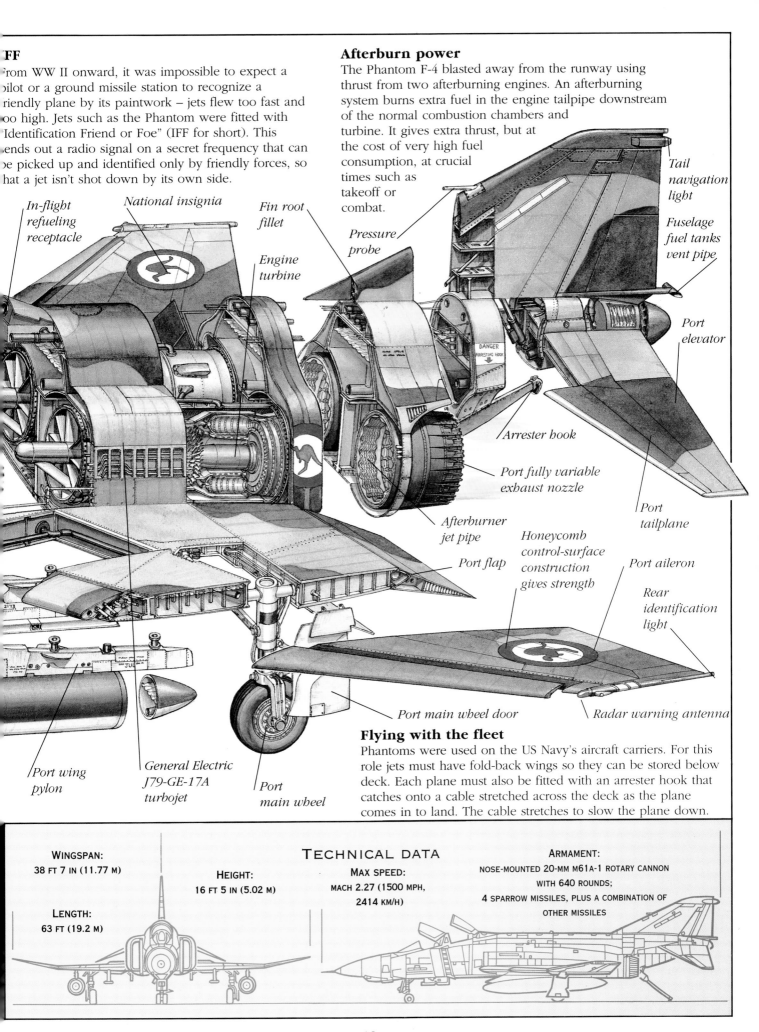

IFF

From WW II onward, it was impossible to expect a pilot or a ground missile station to recognize a friendly plane by its paintwork – jets flew too fast and too high. Jets such as the Phantom were fitted with "Identification Friend or Foe" (IFF for short). This sends out a radio signal on a secret frequency that can be picked up and identified only by friendly forces, so that a jet isn't shot down by its own side.

Afterburn power

The Phantom F-4 blasted away from the runway using thrust from two afterburning engines. An afterburning system burns extra fuel in the engine tailpipe downstream of the normal combustion chambers and turbine. It gives extra thrust, but at the cost of very high fuel consumption, at crucial times such as takeoff or combat.

In-flight refueling receptacle

National insignia

Fin root fillet

Engine turbine

Pressure probe

Tail navigation light

Fuselage fuel tanks vent pipe

Port elevator

Arrester hook

Port fully variable exhaust nozzle

Afterburner jet pipe

Honeycomb control-surface construction gives strength

Port tailplane

Port aileron

Port flap

Rear identification light

Port wing pylon

General Electric J79-GE-17A turbojet

Port main wheel

Port main wheel door

Radar warning antenna

Flying with the fleet

Phantoms were used on the US Navy's aircraft carriers. For this role jets must have fold-back wings so they can be stored below deck. Each plane must also be fitted with an arrester hook that catches onto a cable stretched across the deck as the plane comes in to land. The cable stretches to slow the plane down.

TECHNICAL DATA

WINGSPAN: 38 FT 7 IN (11.77 M)	HEIGHT: 16 FT 5 IN (5.02 M)	MAX SPEED: MACH 2.27 (1500 MPH, 2414 KM/H)	ARMAMENT: NOSE-MOUNTED 20-MM M61A-1 ROTARY CANNON WITH 640 ROUNDS; 4 SPARROW MISSILES, PLUS A COMBINATION OF OTHER MISSILES
LENGTH: 63 FT (19.2 M)			

MIRAGE

IN 1984 THE FRENCH AIR FORCE, THE *ARMÉE DE L'AIR*, took delivery of its first Mirage 2000C. Intended mainly to intercept enemy planes or missiles, its design illustrates some crucial improvements over the first fighter jets made. For modern fighters, maneuverability is much more important than attaining ever-higher speeds. The agile Mirage 2000 can fly at over Mach 2 at high altitude, but it can also perform well at low speeds and can climb rapidly, enabling it to sneak up on a high-altitude target quickly. Armed with powerful radar and computer technology, modern jets like the Mirage take many years to develop. Each plane costs millions to build.

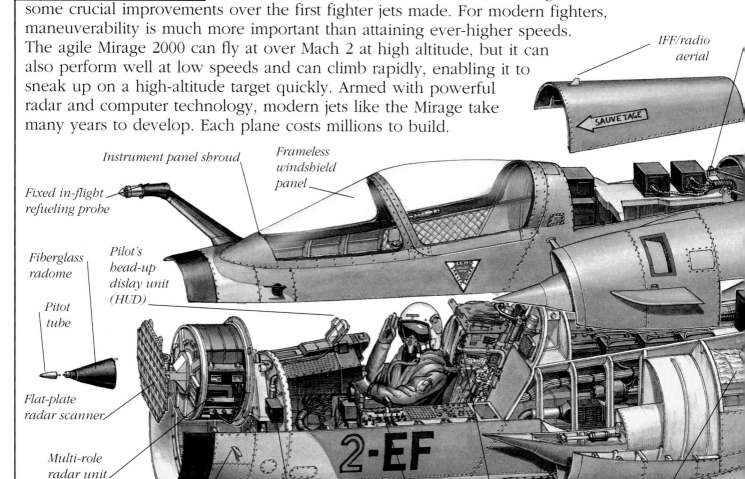

Radio and electronics b

IFF/radio aerial

SAUVETAGE

Instrument panel shroud

Frameless windshield panel

Fixed in-flight refueling probe

Pilot's head-up dislay unit (HUD)

Fiberglass radome

Pitot tube

Flat-plate radar scanner

Multi-role radar unit

Angle of attack probe

Pulse doppler radar unit

Ejection seat

Forward port integral fuel tank

Port side console panel

Landing and taxiing lights

Towing bracket

30-mm DEFA cannon

Fly-by-wire

In an early jet fighter the pilot would pull on a control column and push on rudder-pedals to operate hydraulic systems that moved the plane's control surfaces (parts such as elevons) directly. With a "fly-by-wire" system, the pilot's controls send signals to an on-board computer, and this alters the plane's control surfaces automatically.

TECHNICAL DATA

MAX SPEED: MACH 2.3 (1,520 MPH, 2,445 KM/H)	**HEIGHT:** 11 FT 2 IN (3.4 M)	**ARMAMENT:** 2 X 30-MM DEFA CANNON, COMBINATION OF MISSILES
WINGSPAN: 29 FT 6 IN (9.02 M)	**ENGINE:** SNECMA M53-5 AFTERBURNING TURBOFAN	**LENGTH:** 50 FT 3 IN (15.33 M)

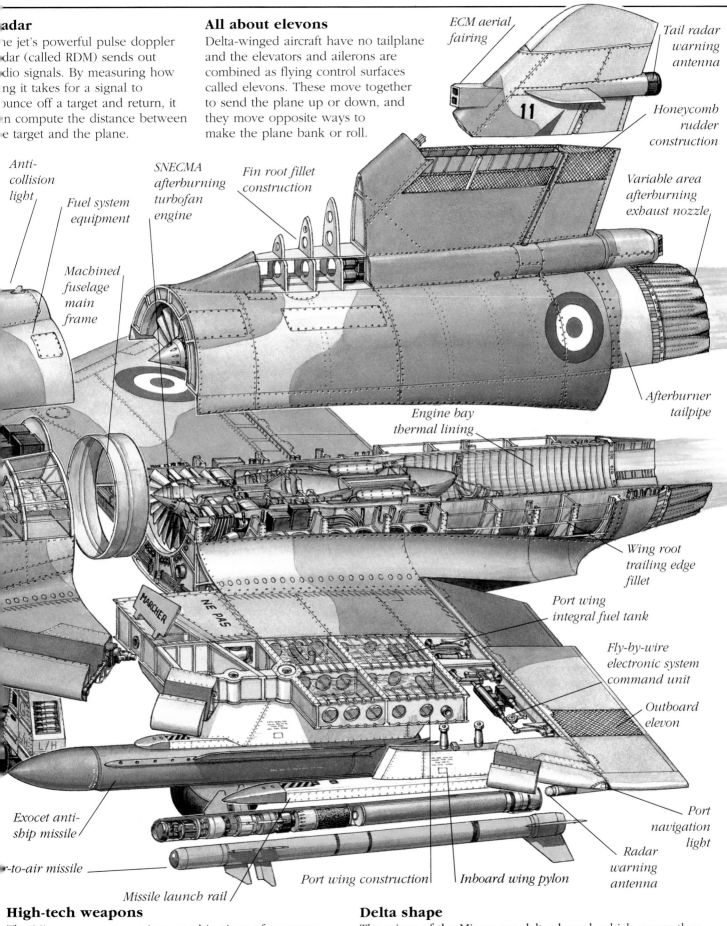

adar

he jet's powerful pulse doppler
dar (called RDM) sends out
dio signals. By measuring how
ng it takes for a signal to
unce off a target and return, it
n compute the distance between
e target and the plane.

All about elevons

Delta-winged aircraft have no tailplane
and the elevators and ailerons are
combined as flying control surfaces
called elevons. These move together
to send the plane up or down, and
they move opposite ways to
make the plane bank or roll.

ECM aerial
fairing

Tail radar
warning
antenna

Honeycomb
rudder
construction

Variable area
afterburning
exhaust nozzle

Anti-
collision
light

Fuel system
equipment

SNECMA
afterburning
turbofan
engine

Fin root fillet
construction

Machined
fuselage
main
frame

Afterburner
tailpipe

Engine bay
thermal lining

Wing root
trailing edge
fillet

Port wing
integral fuel tank

Fly-by-wire
electronic system
command unit

Outboard
elevon

Port
navigation
light

Exocet anti-
ship missile

r-to-air missile

Missile launch rail

Port wing construction

Inboard wing pylon

Radar
warning
antenna

High-tech weapons

The Mirage can carry various combinations of weapons
under its wings and fuselage, including radar-guided or
infrared heat-seeking missiles and laser-guided bombs,
which travel along a laser beam directed at a target.

Delta shape

The wings of the Mirage are delta shaped, which means they
are triangular. They help reduce drag (air resistance) at high
speeds and so increase the airplane's agility. They are smaller
than ordinary wings and more difficult to detect on radar.

F-14A TOMCAT

A GIANT US NAVY AIRCRAFT CARRIER ON A MILITARY exercise springs into action when its fighter jets are ordered into the air to practice defending the fleet from enemy attack. In only a few minutes, a squadron of F-14 fighters is airborne. Since the 1970s, when the first F-14 aircraft versions appeared, this has become a common occurrence. Fast and powerfully armed, F-14's have become the main long-range defense aircraft of the US Navy.

Talking tactics

Like other jet fighters, F-14s fly in groups of at least two. Aircrews may need to talk to each other, but they don't want to give their position away to the enemy. They use secure radio links that are very hard to locate or jam.

Super system

F-14As were followed by F-14D Super Tomcats, with more powerful engines and radar capable of tracking 24 targets.

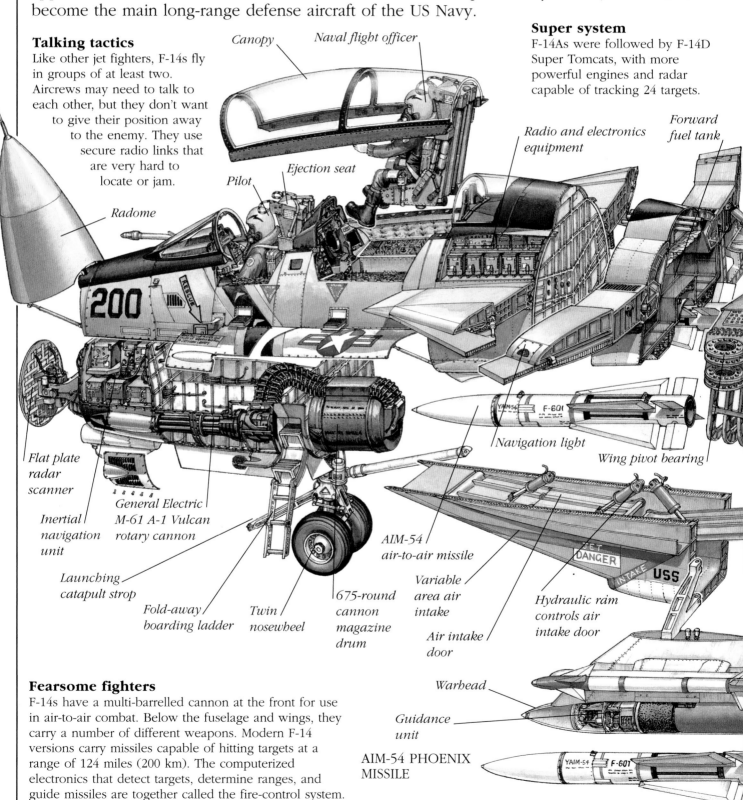

Canopy

Naval flight officer

Forward fuel tank

Radio and electronics equipment

Ejection seat

Pilot

Radome

Flat plate radar scanner

Inertial navigation unit

General Electric M-61 A-1 Vulcan rotary cannon

Launching catapult strop

Fold-away boarding ladder

Twin nosewheel

675-round cannon magazine drum

AIM-54 air-to-air missile

Variable area air intake

Air intake door

Navigation light

Wing pivot bearing

Hydraulic ram controls air intake door

Warhead

Guidance unit

AIM-54 PHOENIX MISSILE

Fearsome fighters

F-14s have a multi-barrelled cannon at the front for use in air-to-air combat. Below the fuselage and wings, they carry a number of different weapons. Modern F-14 versions carry missiles capable of hitting targets at a range of 124 miles (200 km). The computerized electronics that detect targets, determine ranges, and guide missiles are together called the fire-control system.

TECHNICAL DATA

LENGTH:
61 FT 2 IN (18.89 M)

HEIGHT:
16 FT (4.88 M)

WINGSPAN:
UNSWEPT – 64 FT 1.5 IN (19.45 M)
SWEPT – 38 FT 2.5 IN (11.65 M)

ARMAMENT:
GENERAL ELECTRIC
M-61A-1 20-MM
MULTI-BARREL
VULCAN CANNON;
SPARROW AND AIM
AIR-TO-AIR MISSILES

MAX SPEED:
MACH 2.34 (1,564 MPH, 517 KM/HR)

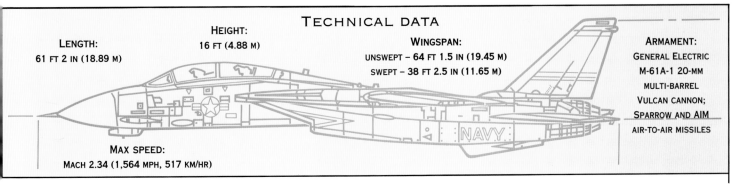

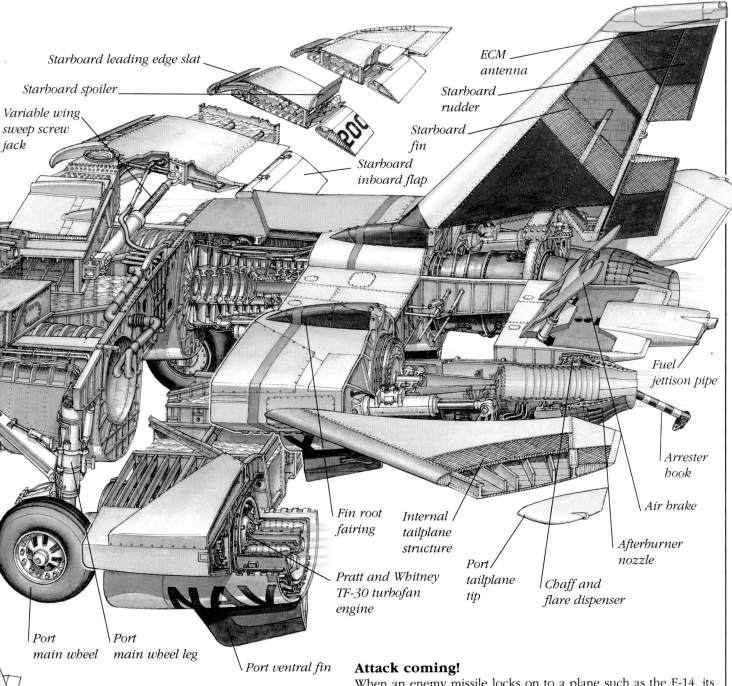

Starboard leading edge slat

Starboard spoiler

Variable wing sweep screw jack

ECM antenna

Starboard rudder

Starboard fin

Starboard inboard flap

Fuel jettison pipe

Arrester hook

Air brake

Afterburner nozzle

Fin root fairing

Internal tailplane structure

Port tailplane tip

Chaff and flare dispenser

Pratt and Whitney TF-30 turbofan engine

Port main wheel

Port main wheel leg

Port ventral fin

Swing wing

The Tomcat is a "variable geometry," or "swing-wing," aircraft, which means it can change its shape by sweeping its wings backward. The onboard computerized flight control system alters the plane's outline in this way to change its performance in the air.

Attack coming!

When an enemy missile locks on to a plane such as the F-14, its equipment emits a radar signal that gives the plane's position away. The F-14 may be armed with anti-radiation missiles that can home in on that enemy signal. If not, that pilot could try to fly out of range, or operate his chaff and flare dispenser. This sends out flares to confuse heat-seeking missiles, and a plume of metal particles (chaff) that hang in the air and fool an enemy missile, directing it away from the plane.

SAAB VIGGEN

IF AN ENEMY WAS EVER TO THREATEN SWEDEN, one of the world's most formidable fighter jets, the Saab Viggen JA37, would emerge from underground hangars dotted around the country. The Viggen, the Swedish word for "thunderbolt," is a multi-role jet, which means it can do several different jobs. Most importantly, it doesn't require a big airfield. It is designed for STOL (short take off and landing) on runways or stretches of road hidden in the thick Scandinavian forests.

Stopping fast

As soon as the plane's nosewheel touches the ground on landing, a thrust-reverser cuts into the turbofan engine. This deflects the exhaust forward through nozzles in the fuselage, helping brake the plane quickly. It's possible to land a JA37 on a slippery, ice-covered runway only 1,640 ft (500 m) long.

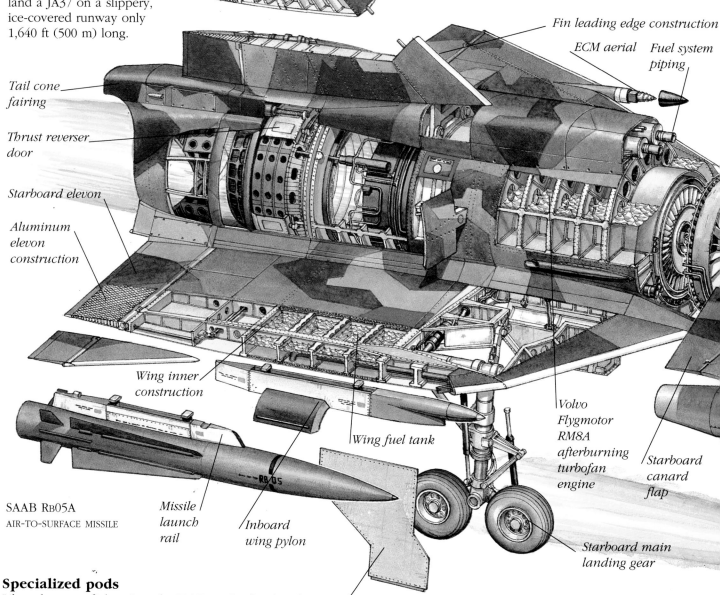

Fin leading edge construction

ECM aerial

Fuel system piping

Tail cone fairing

Thrust reverser door

Starboard elevon

Aluminum elevon construction

Wing inner construction

Wing fuel tank

Volvo Flygmotor RM8A afterburning turbofan engine

Starboard canard flap

SAAB RB05A
AIR-TO-SURFACE MISSILE

Missile launch rail

Inboard wing pylon

Starboard main landing gear

Starboard main landing gear door

Specialized pods

Like other new fighter jets, the JA37 can be fitted with different types of equipment carried in pods under the fuselage. For instance, a reconnaissance version might carry a pod full of cameras, while a ground attack version might be fitted with a pod full of electronic equipment to guide bombs and jam enemy signals.

Fewer planes, same work

Because of their up-to-date radar and weaponry, a pair of modern jets such as Viggens can do the work of a whole squadron of earlier jet fighters.

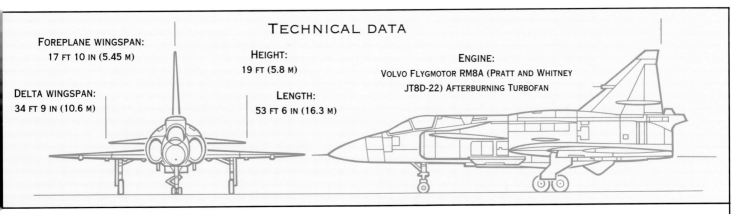

FOREPLANE WINGSPAN:
17 FT 10 IN (5.45 M)

DELTA WINGSPAN:
34 FT 9 IN (10.6 M)

HEIGHT:
19 FT (5.8 M)

LENGTH:
53 FT 6 IN (16.3 M)

ENGINE:
VOLVO FLYGMOTOR RM8A (PRATT AND WHITNEY
JT8D-22) AFTERBURNING TURBOFAN

Foreplanes and fin

The Viggen has a large delta wing and foreplanes called canards. They give the plane extra lift to help it rise up quickly and improve maneuverability as it takes off in a short space. The tailfin can fold down so the plane can be stored somewhere with a low roof. Some Viggen hangars are in underground caves.

The cockpit of the future

In the Viggen cockpit three electronic displays give the pilot information without requiring any head movement. Designers of modern jets are also trying to cut down on tiring arm movements. In the most up-to-date models, all the switches and buttons a pilot needs are located on the control column.

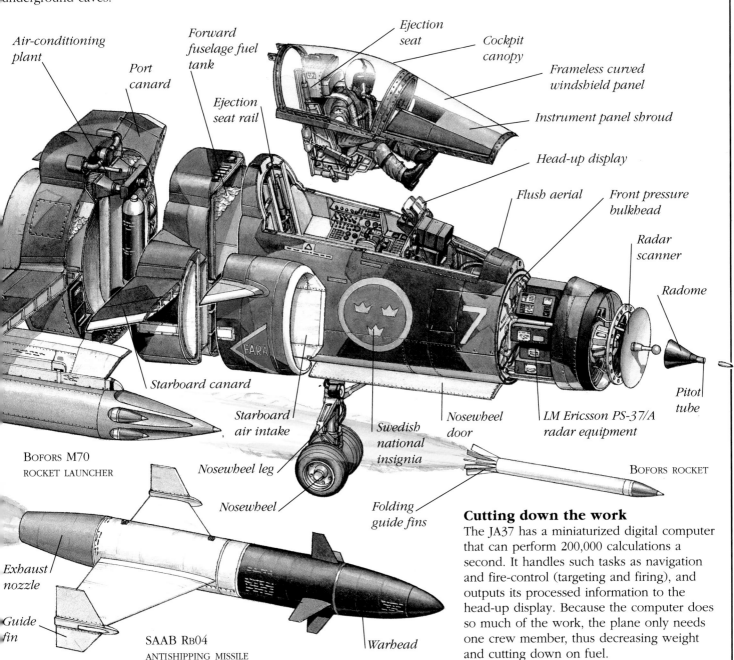

Air-conditioning plant

Port canard

Forward fuselage fuel tank

Ejection seat rail

Ejection seat

Cockpit canopy

Frameless curved windshield panel

Instrument panel shroud

Head-up display

Flush aerial

Front pressure bulkhead

Radar scanner

Radome

Starboard canard

Starboard air intake

Nosewheel leg

Swedish national insignia

Nosewheel door

LM Ericsson PS-37/A radar equipment

Pitot tube

Nosewheel

Folding guide fins

BOFORS ROCKET

BOFORS M70
ROCKET LAUNCHER

Exhaust nozzle

Guide fin

SAAB RB04
ANTISHIPPING MISSILE

Warhead

Cutting down the work

The JA37 has a miniaturized digital computer that can perform 200,000 calculations a second. It handles such tasks as navigation and fire-control (targeting and firing), and outputs its processed information to the head-up display. Because the computer does so much of the work, the plane only needs one crew member, thus decreasing weight and cutting down on fuel.

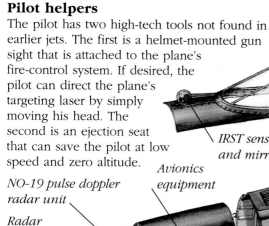

MIG-29 FULCRUM

AT THE BRITISH FARNBOROUGH AIR SHOW IN 1988, amazed aviation experts got their first glimpse of the Russian MiG-29. They could hardly believe their eyes as they watched it perform aerobatics that should have been impossible for any fighter jet. It could unexpectedly stop in midair, leaving a chasing enemy plane zipping helplessly past its quarry. The MiG-29 is one of the most agile fighters in the skies, with a range of technological ideas that will continue to be incorporated in new airplane designs.

Pilot helpers

The pilot has two high-tech tools not found in earlier jets. The first is a helmet-mounted gun sight that is attached to the plane's fire-control system. If desired, the pilot can direct the plane's targeting laser by simply moving his head. The second is an ejection seat that can save the pilot at low speed and zero altitude.

Head-up display

Cockpit canopy

High-frequency aerial

Avionics equipment bay

IRST sensor and mirror

Avionics equipment

NO-19 pulse doppler radar unit

Radar scanner

Radome

Angle of attack transmitter

UHF aerial

Cannon muzzle

Forward fuselage chine fairing

GSh-301 30-mm cannon

Cannon bay air vent

Upper surface air intake doors

ECM aerial panel

Guide fin

Warhead

R-27R1 MEDIUM-RANGE RADAR-GUIDED AIR-TO-AIR MISSILE

Guidance unit

Missile fuselage

Magic eye

When a fighter searches the sky with its radar and locks on to a target, it gives its own position away to the enemy. Not so with the MiG-29. Ahead of the cockpit is a glass ball with a mirror inside. The mirror rotates, scanning the sky for thermal signatures (infrared heat given out by objects). It is called an IRST (Infrared Search and Track) and it hunts silently, giving out no signals of its own. It is linked to the rest of the fire-control system, so once it finds a target, the plane can attack quickly. The MiG also has conventional radar for ground targets or enemy planes hiding in clouds, which the IRST can't spot.

Guidance unit

Guide fin

R-73E SHORT-RANGE, INFRARED OR RADAR-GUIDED AIR-TO-AIR MISSILE

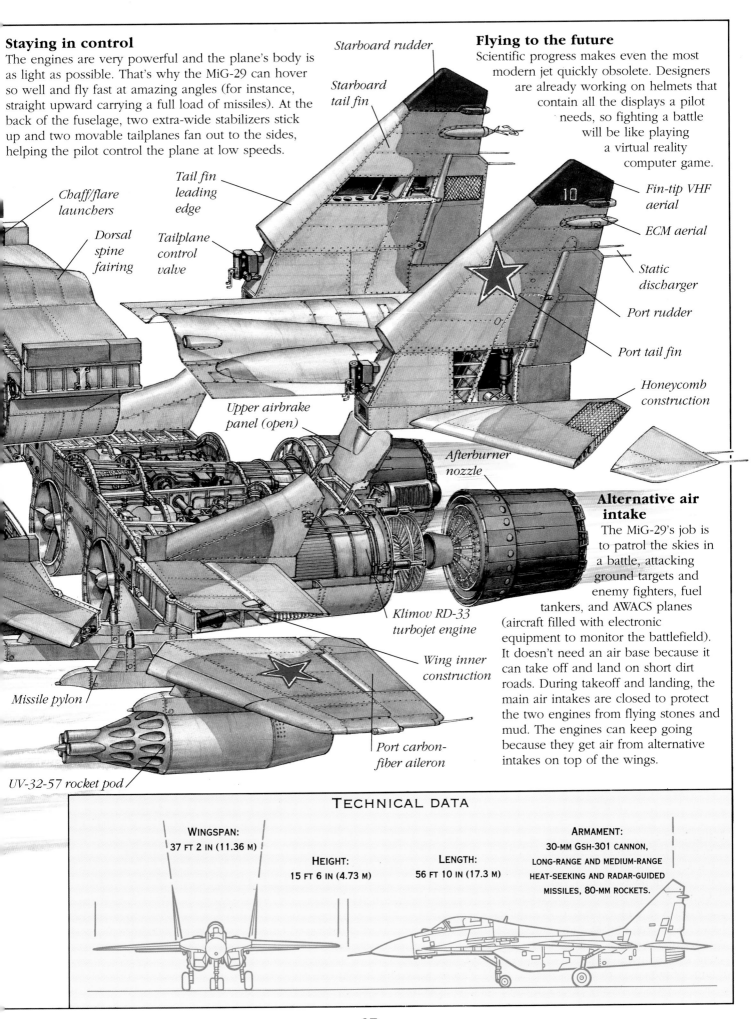

Staying in control

The engines are very powerful and the plane's body is as light as possible. That's why the MiG-29 can hover so well and fly fast at amazing angles (for instance, straight upward carrying a full load of missiles). At the back of the fuselage, two extra-wide stabilizers stick up and two movable tailplanes fan out to the sides, helping the pilot control the plane at low speeds.

Starboard rudder

Starboard tail fin

Flying to the future

Scientific progress makes even the most modern jet quickly obsolete. Designers are already working on helmets that contain all the displays a pilot needs, so fighting a battle will be like playing a virtual reality computer game.

Chaff/flare launchers

Tail fin leading edge

Dorsal spine fairing

Tailplane control valve

Fin-tip VHF aerial

ECM aerial

Static discharger

Port rudder

Port tail fin

Honeycomb construction

Upper airbrake panel (open)

Afterburner nozzle

Alternative air intake

The MiG-29's job is to patrol the skies in a battle, attacking ground targets and enemy fighters, fuel tankers, and AWACS planes (aircraft filled with electronic equipment to monitor the battlefield). It doesn't need an air base because it can take off and land on short dirt roads. During takeoff and landing, the main air intakes are closed to protect the two engines from flying stones and mud. The engines can keep going because they get air from alternative intakes on top of the wings.

Klimov RD-33 turbojet engine

Wing inner construction

Missile pylon

Port carbon-fiber aileron

UV-32-57 rocket pod

TECHNICAL DATA

WINGSPAN:
37 FT 2 IN (11.36 M)

HEIGHT:
15 FT 6 IN (4.73 M)

LENGTH:
56 FT 10 IN (17.3 M)

ARMAMENT:
30-MM GSH-301 CANNON,
LONG-RANGE AND MEDIUM-RANGE
HEAT-SEEKING AND RADAR-GUIDED
MISSILES, 80-MM ROCKETS.

GLOSSARY

Afterburner
A part at the back of an afterburning jet engine. Inside the afterburner extra air is burnt with more fuel to boost the engine's power.

Ailerons
Moveable flying-control surfaces on airplane wings that help keep a plane stable in the air. They control banking and rolling.

Air intake
The opening at the front of a jet engine. Air is drawn in here to feed the jet engines.

Anti-radiation missile
A missile that locks on to signals emitted by enemy radar stations.

Delta shaped canard

Camouflage
Colored paintwork on an airplane that hides it from enemy view. The colors and patterns vary. For instance, if a plane works over desert areas it is likely to be painted a sandy color. In wooded country it is likely to be green and brown.

Chaff
Metal particles that a plane can shoot out behind it. They hang in the air to attract an enemy radar-guided missile away from the plane itself.

Combustion chamber
A space inside an engine where fuel and air are mixed and burned.

Compressor
A series of metal vanes that spin around inside the front of a jet engine. They draw in air and squeeze as much of it as possible into the engine's next stage, the combustion chamber.

Control surfaces
The various wing and tail flaps that make a plane dive, climb, pitch, yaw, or roll.

Delta wing

Delta wing
A triangular-shaped wing that reduces air resistance at high speeds.

ECM
Initials standing for **Electronic Counter-Measures** – equipment that can jam enemy radar signals.

Elevators
Movable flaps at the tail of an airplane. They can put the plane into a dive or climb.

Elevons
Wing flying control surfaces on a delta-wing plane that has no tail. They combine the jobs of elevators and ailerons.

Fire-control systems
Equipment for targeting, aiming, and firing weapons.

Flying suit
A pilot's outfit, designed to counteract the effects of acceleration forces on the body. If the pilot ejects, it will protect him from cold, and it sometimes contains a waterproof "immersion suit" layer in case the pilot ditches in water.

FLYING SUIT

Fitted helmet or "bone dome"

Oxygen mask

Immersion suit layer

Oxygen supply hose

Life jacket

Map pocket

"Anti-g" trousers

Flying boots

Fly-by-wire
Electronic computerized controls that automatically adjust the various wing and tail flaps on a plane.

Fuselage
The central body of an airplane.

"g"
A measurement of acceleration due to gravity – the force that pulls downward on an airplane as it climbs upward from the Earth's surface.

Ground control
Controllers on the ground who organize and oversee a plane on a mission.

HUD
Initials standing for **head-up display** – the projection of vital information onto the windshield in front of a pilot.

Heat-seeking missile
A missile that locates and locks on to heat emitted by enemy aircraft.

Helmet-up display
All the information that a pilot needs, projected inside his helmet, right in front of his eyes.

IFF
Initials standing for **Identification Friend or Foe** – a signal on a secret frequency that can only be recognized by friendly forces.

IRST
Initials standing for **Infra-red Search and Track.** A jet-fighter mirror system that scans the sky looking for the heat emissions of enemy airplanes.

Laser
A powerful beam of light that can be directed at a target.

Leading edge slats
Control surfaces along the front edge of a wing. These are automatically controlled on modern jets. They help keep the plane stable at low speeds.

Mach number
A way of comparing speed through the air to the speed of sound. Mach 1 is the speed at which sound travels at a given altitude. An aircraft traveling at Mach 1 at sea level would be flying at 760.98 mph (1224.67 km/h) at a temperature of 50°F (15°C). Above 36,089 ft (11,000 m), Mach 1 is measured as 659.78 mph (1061.81 km/h).

Nacelle
A streamlined pod containing an engine.

Personal location beacon
A military pilot carries this at all times. If the pilot ejects, it activates and sends out signals on an emergency distress frequency, so the pilot can be found and rescued.

Pitot tube
A tube that sticks out of a plane nose or wing and takes in air as the plane flies along. Attached sensors measure the air pressure to determine the plane's air speed.

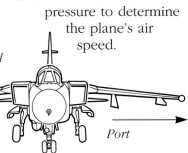

Starboard

Port

Port
Left-hand side of the plane (as the pilot looks out of the cockpit). There is a red navigation light on the port wingtip.

Radar
High-powered radio pulses that are transmitted, bounce off an object, and return to the receiver.

Rudder
A vertical flying-control surface on the tail of a plane.

Starboard
Right-hand side of a plane (as the pilot looks out of the cockpit).There is a green navigation light on the starboard wingtip

STOL
Initials that stand for **Short Take Off and Landing**, used to describe a plane that doesn't need a long runway.

TURBOFAN

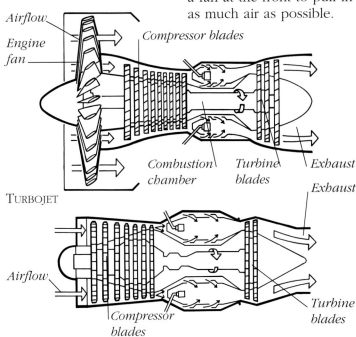

Airflow
Engine fan
Compressor blades
Combustion chamber
Turbine blades
Exhaust
Exhaust
TURBOJET
Airflow
Compressor blades
Turbine blades

Swing wing
(Also called variable geometry wing). A wing that can swing backward and forward to change its shape.

Thermal signature
The measurement of heat given out by an object.

Turbine
A series of curved metal blades that spin around like a windmill. In a jet engine, exhaust gases spin a turbine, which, in turn drives a compressor around.

Turbofan
A turbojet engine that uses a fan at the front to pull in as much air as possible.

Turbojet
A jet engine which uses a compressor to feed air into a combustion chamber where it is mixed with fuel and ignited to create thrust.

VTOL
Initials standing for **Vertical Take Off and Landing,** used to describe a plane that can rise straight up into the air or descend straight down on a runway.

Thrust directed downward from jet engine lifts aircraft

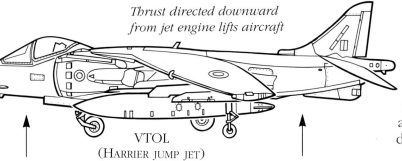

VTOL
(HARRIER JUMP JET)

INDEX

Acknowledgments

DK would like to thank the
following people who helped
with the preparation of
this book:

Gary Biggin for line artworks
Lynn Bresler for the index
Constance Novis for editorial support
Paul Wood for DTP design